To:

Everyone deserves

to be

IN -LOVE

Printed in the United States of America

ISBN 978-1502992024

Your Dream Love Awaits You....

Acknowledgements

I would like to thank my grandparents Walter and Mary Coleman and James and Faylese Herd for getting married. When I reminisce about my childhood I remember looking at pictures when they were young and how their beautiful wedding pictures caught my attention. I did not understand it then, but looking at those pictures as a kid, it was a pictorial blueprint of what made the continuing generations of our family so strong; *marriage*. I also thank my mother and father, uncles and aunts, and older cousins who either are married or have been married. The relationships have not always lasted but that does not take away the 15, 20, and 30+ years they invested in one another. I am truly appreciative to you all for challenging my generation's reluctance to marriage, my own *playerish* ways, and showing me the power of relationships. Thank you and I love you.

I send a special thank you to my wife, Makalia Francis-Coleman, for editing this book.

Contents

INTRODUCTION

"Marriage!?! You mean, me, get married? Nope, I don't think so. Maybe when I'm 50 years old or something but not right now." Those were my words at 23 years of age. Within the next three years of making that statement I was married and happier than I had ever been in my life.

I have not written this book to educate women about how to find a man exactly like me or men to find a woman exactly like my wife. This book is to help men and women gain awareness about relationship dynamics that I believe are important at the beginning of a relationship with a person who is *right for YOU*. The information within this text will also be informative for those individuals and couples who are several years into a relationship.

This is not a book specifically for one gender. All readers will benefit from this reading in a way that inspires them to become better at living a fulfilling life with their better half. My goal is to give you some themes and insight from my own perspective to help you during the beginning process of meeting your life-partner. Grab some paper and a pen as you prepare to take a trip through your past, present, and into your future.

Chapter 1 - YOUR CONVERSATION

A person's conversation tends to be indicative of their developmental stage. Psychologist Erik Erikson breaks down life into eight stages which he calls psychosocial development. For example, most American teens are interested in video games, girls/boys, some mischievousness, etc. Middle-age adulthood garners different interests. "Erikson observed that middle-age is when we tend to be occupied with creative and meaningful work and with issues surrounding our family," (ARLENE F. HARDER, 2011). The same goes for the other six stages of life. My point for introducing these stages is to address that your interest and desires may differ during certain periods and stages of life which will influence your level of conversation and the things you talk about. At 23 years of age I was still engaging in some of the same things I was engaging in at 17 years old and 19 years old; partying, sex, fighting random people, and hanging out with my friends (Erikson might have stated that I was stuck in my adolescent stage). Other than work, those four things saturated most of my time. My conversations consisted of those things as well. "Yo Mike, what are we doing tonight bruh?" "The same thing we do every night Shawn; drinkin' and inviting broads over," Mike would reply. Sometimes I was the center of my friend Dre or Terrence's conversation at a party. "Shawn beat that dude's ass yo. The dude was runnin' his mouth too much so Shawn handled his biz."

Though I have always attracted different types of females from different races, cultures, and socioeconomic backgrounds, the reason they were interested in me was the same. They saw a tall, handsome male with no self-control and unfortunately many of those girls/women thought that it was sexy. I recall a time in which a big brawl broke out at a night club. I really didn't feel like fighting so I grabbed the girl, I took her to a safe area, and waited for the fight to end. When I did that, she looked surprised as if I had made the wrong decision. Later that night in the car she said "I thought you would have jumped in the fight. I heard you were crazy like that." I found myself having to rationalize why I made a sane decision. It was as if she wanted me to live up to my "legend", even if it meant jail or death. Like I said, most females at that time enjoyed being around *the wild me*. Don't get me wrong, there were a few females in my life who were more sophisticated than the majority of the young ladies but even they had a moderate liking for my aggressive nature.

When it came to the women I talked to, we rarely had conversations about life or anything of substance. Conversations consisted of drinking, partying, and other *adult activities*. One particular young lady would text me the same thing every other day; "What's up...?". "Chillin", I'd reply. "Can I come over?", she'd text back. "Yea." That was it. That was our relationship.

I was a twenty-three year old, no-tact-having, aggressive, womanizer. Ironically, this was when I met my wife, Makalia. On the surface, she was just like the other girls I had been talking to; very pretty and fun. But, she had different conversations, hated my aggressive tendencies and was repugnant with the way I behaved when I lacked self-control. Where other females were stimulated and excited by my rage and aggression, she was embarrassed by it. I remember riding in my 1991 black Honda Accord coupe and she inquired about why I acted the way I did. "What makes you act like a wild boar in public, Shawn?" I thought for a few seconds and then responded, "I don't know, people just make me mad."

"People can't _make_ you do anything. All they can do is trigger you. You need to stop acting like that when you get upset. Have you ever tried thinking about your future and what might happen if your anger gets the best of you one day?"

"Yea, sometimes..."

"You need to think, Shawn."

I could hear my mother in her voice. This girl was offering solutions to my anger problems. This was not normal for me. This girl had _different conversation_. What is your conversation like?

Chapter 2 - THE POWER OF YOUR EXPECTATIONS

Now that I am aware of the power of a woman stating what she will accept and what she will not accept in a relationship, I am surprised that more women (younger women particularly) do not do it. If a woman wants to weed out the scrubs from the potential husbands, she will need to periodically and consistently communicate her expectations early in the relationship, make her partner aware of what is acceptable and what is not, and maintain a robust allegiance with her morals and standards. Your partner should have his own set of standards and expectations as well so that you both can assess where the other person stands.

I believe **both parties** should be faithful to one another at all times. Ladies, do not accept a man who expects you to allow him to have random sex partners. That is not true love and it is disrespectful. If you and your partner enjoy that type of thing and you have an agreement, that's one thing but I do not believe that it will garner a fully happy relationship steeped in true love. I have found that about 70% of the women I talked to before my wife never communicated their expectations to me. It was strictly about physical attraction. About 28% of these young ladies gave me some inclination regarding what they wanted from me but what they wanted *should have not been* communicated. For example, some of these women would say things like "I don't mind you talking to other girls. Just let me come through when I want to come over." I remember one young lady told me, "You should use me as your late night call until you find a girlfriend." (Most of the young women I refer to in this book, I did not have sex with.) The unfortunate thing about this is that they were actually setting themselves up to be woman #2 or woman #3 without us ever having sex. I do not boast about any of this, as I have not ever been a braggadocios type of person. I write like this to be transparent and educational.

Many men tend to have multiple sex partners. Women do not need to contribute to a man's lack of sexual self-control. More importantly, women need to stop accepting the notion that all men cheat. When you say this you are creating the idea that it will be accepted and some men will develop the faulty belief that cheating is part of normal relationships. Women, STOP!

You may be thinking, *what about the 2% of women?* Only a select few showed me that they had standards and morals that they, for the most part, would not budge on. They often communicated what they would accept and what they would not accept. In the beginning of our relationship, my wife was aware that I talked to a few other girls and she constantly said to me, "I'm not being one of your girls, Shawn. You decide what you want to do by this date or I'm done." I remember another time shortly before going back home to the Virgin Islands for a holiday, she said, "I'm going back home to the islands for a month. If I get back and you haven't decided between me and them, I'm done." **That is how a woman is supposed to use the power of her expectations**. Within two weeks of meeting my wife I knew that she was someone I could spend my life with. I also believe that she knew how I felt about her and as she started to feel the same about me, she increased her intensity about communicating her expectations in order to get what she wanted. I knew that I loved Makalia but I was not sure about what I wanted. Prior to meeting her, I had no reason to think about a serious relationship. Sometimes one partner may be content with the current state of the relationship while the other is envisioning the future. This is not to say that the content person does not care to grow the relationship, it may be that the person is not thinking about the future as yet. In my case, Makalia's expectations made me aware of what she wanted from the relationship and caused me to think about my own future. That was a powerful time and it was the nudge I needed to stimulate growth in our relationship. *Her ultimatum in addition to me realizing I was in love with her caused me to understand the seriousness that I had to choose.* Though the choice was easy for me to make it may not have happened if she did not *communicate her expectations.*

If you are in a relationship with a person who is nonchalantly going through the motions like I was at the beginning of my relationship, it may be advantageous for you to put the person in a situation where they have to choose what he/she wants. Depending on the dynamics and the genuineness of the relationship, this is a point where the relationship can grow in a healthy direction or both individuals depart. Whether you choose to **grow** or **go**, the decision should eliminate any chance of you wasting precious time.

Here is another note that you ladies might like too; years after, Makalia used this same method (*communicating her expectations*) to get me to start thinking about marriage. "Shawn," she'd say while looking into my eyes. "I'm not just going to be your girlfriend for years and years." I'm thinking to myself *Damn girl! You play to win huh?!?* (lol). Find your power and utilize it by communicating your expectations.

Chapter 3 - NICE THINGS

Nice things are just that...nice. Well, they are also expensive. In high school kids were caught up and fixated on brand name clothes, shoes, purses, and hats. If you didn't wear Ralph Lauren, FUBU, BOSS, Polo, Tommy Hilfiger, Nike, Adidas, or other brand names that were *in* at the time, you were considered poor, broke, and unpopular. The funny thing is, the poorest kids in school wore those clothes (overcompensating for what they actually did not have) and ended up being unpopular later in life where the truly elite people begin to grow and excel. People like nice things but many people do not go about obtaining and maintaining these things in a humble way. *Many people feel the need to advertise the things they purchase not realizing that showing off may come at an even higher cost.* Some people who procure nice things and then boast about it end up paying for it in the long run because a truly humble person (a "good" man or woman), is turned off by these arrogant gestures. Do not allow your love for materialistic things to block you from materializing a relationship with the love of your life; Mr. or Mrs. Right.

When Makalia and I met, I was a bit hesitant to get serious with her because she always wore designer things and from the outside she appeared to be a high maintenance girl. One day when I went to pick her up from her house for a date I noticed she was wearing a pair of shoes I really liked. "Those must of cost a lot huh?", I sarcastically asked. "Nope, only eight dollars," she replied. "Eight dollars!?!" I loudly asked again, as if there was no way this high maintenance chick was telling me the truth. She looked at me with a serious face and said, "What? I can't wear eight dollar shoes?"

"I guess you can," I responded.

"If I like a pair of shoes I'll buy them. I don't care if they're eight dollars or $800."

When she said that to me, she gained about 150 cool points in my book. It was not a case of me being cheap and not wanting to kick out cash for nice things but prior to that statement I thought I was possibly getting into a relationship with a potential gold digger. I was not sure which girl on "Coming to America" she was; Lisa McDowell or Patrice McDowell. I wanted no part of Patrice but I could deal with Lisa. I wanted a woman that could wear high heels and an expensive dress but also didn't mind putting on old sneakers and a t-shirt to run some errands. [No disrespect toward the women in the communities I have grown up in but I am <u>not</u> referring to a completely nonchalant woman who goes to the grocery store in a shower cap and pajamas.] Makalia's apparent high class beauty appealed to my eyes but her lack of need to have every brand new purse, shoe, bag, pair of earrings, etc., showed me her *high class quality as a human being* and that attracted me more. I was impressed that she was a woman that had nice things but chose to not always need expensive things. Do you like nice things? Do you absolutely need to have nice things? What is that saying about you…or better yet what is your dream partner interpreting when they see that in you?

Chapter 4 - THE TWO-WEEK SLEEP OVER

Whose tooth brush is this? Whose sweater is this? Why are high heels in my closet? These are some of the questions that I asked myself when I came home to my apartment after work. I was a single bachelor but I kept finding women's clothes and items in my apartment and I knew they were not mine! At this point I realized that Makalia had been staying with me periodically for several days at a time. Two days here, three days there, and sometimes she would stay for *two weeks*. It was not that she did not have her own place. She actually had a very nice place in Mt. Washington, Pittsburgh, Pa. For some reason however, she began staying with me for extended periods of time. Usually I would have been very uncomfortable with this because I loved my own space. I did let some women stay over from time to time but I did not like them staying over too much because I did not want to get attached to anyone. I cannot speak for anyone else but unconsciously (and maybe consciously) I did not want to feel an emotional or intimate connection with anyone outside of my family. I did not want to be responsible for contributing to a healthy relationship with anyone other than God, myself, and my family. To be more direct, I did not want to experience or deal with the separation anxiety that came whenever Makalia would leave to go to work or back to her house. I believe that this is a phenomenon that many men fear when it comes to commitment; we just do not talk about it much. It was different when it came to Makalia, who I was just dating. I did not mind her staying over. Actually, I liked her company. No, I loved her company. This was a great indicator that she was someone that I could make a *real girlfriend*. I did not have some of the concerns with her as I did with some of the other girls. I was not concerned that she would be messy and make my apartment a daily wreck. I was not concerned that she would steal or bring random people into my house if and when I was gone. I was not concerned in-general that our lifestyles would clash. She had a great deal of my trust and it appeared to be a result of her staying with me for extended periods of time. This caused me to believe that I could spend a lifetime with her.

Chapter 5 - YOUR FAMILIAR SPIRIT

In counseling psychology there is a term called *transference* in which someone responds to person A as if they are person B because person A reminds them so much of person B that they no longer see person A as being person A. Everyone at some point in their life experiences transference of some sort with someone. Have you ever met someone who reminded you so much of somebody else that it almost seemed like you had known them for several years? You were probably *familiar with their spirit*. Sometimes it can be such a strong connection that it may stymie you from realizing how you are interacting with the person. Thus the term transference in which you are transferring the energy of how you interact with person B onto person A.

When I met my wife I began to realize that she reminded me of my mother. Her facial expressions, her idiosyncrasies, even her scent...almost everything she did reminded me of my mother. I remember one time in particular when my wife and I were laying on my couch in my apartment back when we began dating. From the positioning of how she was holding me, to her scent, I actually thought for a moment that I was 12 years old again laying in my mother's arms for a nap. It was as if I was already spiritually programmed to be attracted to Makalia. I was familiar with her spirit.

Here is the flip side to familiarity with someone's spirit. Sometimes person A, who means well, has to deal with misplaced anger, negativity, etc., that has nothing to do with them but everything to do with person B.

They say that boys tend to marry their mothers, and girls marry their fathers. For example, the relationship I have had with my mother has been tumultuous at times. There are things about her that cause me to distance myself from her and I anticipate that she may feel the same about me. Since my wife reminded me so much of my mother, an innocuous facial expression, comment, or gesture caused me to avoid interactions with her. Her behavior would irritate me in the same way my mother's behavior did. I recommend parents and couples to explore how your parenting style is influencing your child's choice of a future partner and/or how your upbringing has influenced the choice of your current partner and the relationship you have with each other. I truly believe that my wife Makalia is my soul mate and I am glad that she has some of the nurturing qualities my mother has. At the same time, I have had to do a great deal of work to overcome my feelings about her resembling-characteristics to my mom that I do not like. This is one of the steps in our marital process that we still work on as we continue to grow with one another.

I am sure that there is a large cohort of people who have chosen to marry an unfamiliar spirit. For example, let's say I would have chosen not to enter a relationship with Makalia with the attitude "Oh hell no! You remind me of my mom. I don't want any part of you," (I'm sure there are people who do that). That decision, whether done consciously or unconsciously is still based on how you feel/felt about a familiar spirit. Thus, whether your partner has a familiar or unfamiliar spirit there will still be work to do.

Years after I got married to Makalia, I had an opportunity to speak to a very hard working and brilliant young woman who I had engaged in a sexual relationship with. The young woman asked me "Why didn't you choose me?" I was a bit shocked by the question because 1) I was too humble to think that she or any woman (even my wife) would desire me as a boyfriend, let alone a husband and 2) she never *communicated her expectations* and told me that she wanted anything more than what we were doing. I told that young woman both of those things but I also told her that the main reason was that I was more familiar with the spirit and the energy of Makalia. The young woman was and still appears to be an incredible woman. It was not solely reasons #1 and #2 that caused me to go in a different direction relationship-wise. It was my attraction to a more *familiar spirit*.

Chapter 6 - TIMELINESS OF HYGIENE

When I refer to hygiene I am not simply talking about making sure that you shower and smell good. I am referring to the timeliness in which you choose to engage in showers, baths, washing your clothes, cleaning your room, and things of that nature. Everyone can take a shower but not everyone chooses to take one every day or right after a jog. In my 29 years of life, I have not yet read an article or met a woman who said "I just love when a man goes three or four days without showering." Most women do not think that it's sexy and when women do it it's not attractive to us either. If my wife were to make a habit out of going to play a game of tennis, then coming home to lounge around the house, then putting on a different set of clothes (without showering) to go to the movies, she would not be my wife. I can understand a few times here and there when that may happen, but to have that be a women's modus operandi is awkward to me and a little gross. If she did that type of thing at the beginning of our relationship that would surely be a deal breaker for me. Thank God that my wife does not do things like that. She has always had great hygiene but her attention and *timeliness to her hygiene* is something I noticed and really gained an appreciation for. No matter what activity we were out doing, as soon as we returned home she made sure that we both washed our hands. We can't touch anything in the house (including each other) without washing our hands first. When she got home from work, she would wash her hands, give me a kiss, hop in the shower, and then come downstairs to cuddle and interact with me. It is not that she had OCD. She just wanted to be fresh…and I like that. Pay attention to the *timeliness of your hygiene*.

Chapter 7 - INTELLIGENCE

Without denigrating my own level of intelligence, I have always been honest regarding my mediocre academic abilities. I received honor and high honor roll until the eighth grade but high school and college proved to be a very difficult experience for me academically. However, I was able to regain a robust performance with my grades when I entered the master's level. In high school and college I was always amazed when my classmates took notes in unison while I was sitting looking at the teacher. It was as if everyone in the class but me knew what the teacher had planned to put on the test. For a long time I truly believed that my classmates and all of my teachers were having some sort of secret meeting before and after class without me. All throughout school I struggled to comprehend the text book readings. I felt so inferior to other kids in class who could read a book, write an excellent book review and/or pass the test that was based on the reading – right after reading the book. I always wanted to be like those students. In order for me to barely get a B in some classes, I had to read the book, go online and read summaries about the book and watch the movie. In some cases I literally had to contact the author just to get a strong understanding of the content. Sometimes this is still the case today. Though I have not been as academically adept as some of my peers throughout my educational career, I no longer believe that I am not as intelligent. I have creative intelligence. I have the ability to utilize creative ways (though it may take longer) to learn what others may be able to learn in a shorter amount of time. Furthermore, because I have to learn the same thing so many different ways, I tend to have an advantage because I have referenced so many sources.

When I began dating my wife and she continued her *two week sleep overs*, I noticed that she was a reader. I postulate that many of the previous women I talked to before my wife may have been readers too, but because our interactions were so brief, I rarely saw them holding a book and reading one. When I saw my wife reading books time after time and finishing book after book, it took me back to my days of high school and college when I felt inferior to my classmates. That was the point when I realized, yet again, *I would not be able to keep her if I could not keep up with her.* The difference this time was that the combination of seeing her reading book after book, and me not wanting to feel inferior anymore, inspired me to want to become a reader. And I did. I started reading books I liked. Books about life, psychology, boxing, and things like that. Within the fourth book I completed I realized that I had a passion for learning! I was now a reader. Not only was I reading the books and finishing them but I understood them. I started reading books about science, politics, and anything else I could get my hands on. I was so excited and proud of myself that I took advantage of every opportunity I got to talk to my wife about what I was learning in these books. "Hey babe," I would energetically approach her. "Erik Erikson developed this thing called psychosocial development. He believes that people go through different stages of life…Oh! And did you know that scientists have found new planets in the last couple of years!?!" She always responded to me empathetically with love because she didn't want to embarrass me or make me feel stupid. Eventually I realized that her countenance was saying, *Shawn…honey I know everything you're talking about already because I learned it back in high school and college.* My new found passion for learning had caused me to forget that my wife has been a high honor student for her ENTIRE educational career. The things that I had been learning about and re-teaching myself were things that I should have learned five to seven years before if I had been paying attention in school.

I give God all of the praise for my success and my life, which is why I give God total praise for bringing me a wife like Makalia. She has worked every nerve I have ever had but she is truly a miracle to me. I was not expecting any woman to want me as a husband, let alone a woman like her. I can tell you today that the very fact that I have a master's degree and a new found love for reading and learning is a direct result of being around her level of intelligence. I would not be an author today if she did not inspire these new passions in me through her own lifestyle and way of living. The powerful thing about it all is that she probably did not know her contribution to *the new me* until years later when I told her. The point that I am trying to make is not about becoming smarter. The point I am making is that my partner's lifestyle and level of *intelligence* inspired me to <u>better myself</u>. How can you and your partner inspire each other to become better individuals?

Chapter 8 - YOUR VALUE TO THE EMPIRE

Do I love my wife? *Yes.* Am I deeply in love with my wife? *Yes.* Did I marry my wife solely based on me loving her and being in love with her? *Absolutely not.* I have come to the conclusion that marriage is about love but it is also about business. I did not notice it at first but eventually I became conscious of my wife's quality as a woman and as a person. I became conscious of what she brought to the table. She was 21 years old with a bachelor's degree and passionately searching to begin her career towards a bright future. She was also a humble person with morals and came from a good family. She was someone that I could see myself building an empire with, raising a family, and being with for the rest of my life. I do not want to give you the idea that because someone has degrees they are marriage material, nor do I want to cause you to develop the erroneous belief that you should try to live off of someone else's achievements. You need to chase your own dreams, do your own self-work, make your own money, have your own things, etc.

Early on during the beginning of our relationship when my wife and I were talking about moving in together, I was initially against the idea of us living under one roof. I told her that we both needed to be able to fully support ourselves individually then we would know if we would be able to move in together. My thinking was that if she could support herself financially without me and if I could support myself financially without her, once we moved in together, it would create a fortified empire. I know that finances is one of the factors toward relationships falling apart so I did not want to go into our relationship as a couple living together with that burden. I wanted to add *value* to her *empire* and I had already seen that she had the potential to add value to mine.

Chapter 9 - THE ATTRACTION AND VALUE OF WHAT YOU 'DO NOT' BRING TO THE TABLE

I do not believe that it is healthy for people to get into relationships solely based off of what someone else can give or do for them. That happens far too often and the relationship usually goes awry because it never really had a stable foundation. I do believe there is value in what both parties in a relationship may NOT be able to bring to the table and that there can be power and influence regarding the things each party may not (temporarily) be able to do. This is not something that we hear or read about much but it can lead to a healthy and successful relationship.

During the beginning of our relationship, Makalia, like many recent college graduates, was looking for full-time employment outside of the part time job she already had. Her part time job was not providing her with the means to fully support herself in the way she desired. At that time I had a full time job and I was doing fairly well for myself. When we began getting serious I was more than happy to help her get the things she needed; including a better job. They say men are the providers and that might be true because most men enjoy providing things and it makes us feel good. Makalia had a need and I was able to supply her with help, resources, and information to better her quality of life. Though I knew it would not be healthy for her to continue to depend on my financial support, I was *attracted* to and eager to help the person I was falling in love with. There were things I did not bring to the table too…like common sense. Makalia brought a lot of common sense and effective solutions to certain problems I was having in my life. We complemented one another and were able to help increase each other's *value* individually and as a couple. It should also be stated that we have both became self-sufficient in these areas and currently do not need each other in these areas as much as we previously did. As a partner (especially as a provider) you should prepare for the time when your partner does not need you as much as they once did (i.e. financially). This can be a game changer that can cause ruptures in the relationship if there is not open communication, high emotional intelligence, respect, love, and empathy in the way both parties

go about dealing with these changes in relationship dynamics.
Remember that even if your partner may not need you as much
in a certain area it does not mean that they love you any less. It
may simply mean that you have been a great teacher in that area
and that they have grown.

Chapter 10 - YOUR SEX & SEX-APPEAL

I am a direct person and at times throughout my life I have been unaware that my approach, response, and/or reaction to things have offended people. I have chosen not to change who I am but I have chosen to make some adjustments and use more tact. As I write about the topic of this chapter, my goal is to be authentic but remain respectful.

I lost my virginity when I was 16 years old. I do not boast about the types of women I have been with because as I previously stated, that just isn't me. However, I will say (humbly) that throughout my entire life, the women I have shared intimacy with have been beautiful. As a man, I appreciate the beauty of women. Men have told me that they have had a multitude of horrible intimate experiences with women in which the woman's intimacy did not live up to her physical beauty. I have rarely had that experience.

When I speak at high schools and colleges, I constantly meet young people in their teens and early twenties who say that they do not practice safe sex. I cannot understand that. When I engaged in intimate experiences, I enjoyed it but I was not willing to do it unprotected because I was not in a committed relationship with these women and it was unsafe.

This is not something that should be glorified but it is a harsh reality that men do not want to give up being able to enjoy any woman they desire. Men (especially ones like myself) have a strong visual attraction and appreciation for women. I never thought one woman would be able to satisfy me sexually. Then I met Makalia.

My wife is such a lady and it is so adorable to me. As I write this chapter I am trying to find the right words and way to structure them to uphold the ladylike image that my wife truly embodies. She is a high quality person and a woman's woman…but she is also *very creative* and pleasing during our intimate journeys. I understand that certain religious entities emphasize not to have sex before marriage and I AGREE WITH THAT. There are too many sexually transmitted infections and diseases rampant in today's society and too many babies that are not being born out of love to be having sex with someone you have no long term desire to be with. But since this book is a documentary of the data I have personally gleaned through my own eyes and experiences, I must say that Makalia's sex was and still is the best of the best and it had something to do with me wanting to be with her. Not only did it have something to do with me wanting to be with her but *it had everything to do with me discontinuing sexual relationships with women I was involved with when I met her.* I was so into her mentally, emotionally, spiritually, and physically that *there was no reason for me to share an intimate relationship with any other woman.* I only wanted to have that with her.

Having experienced sex with no strings attached vs. sex within someone I am in love with, I have found, for myself at least, there is no comparison. *Sex with random women is fun but sex with the woman you're in love with is FUNOMENAL.* The women before Makalia had great sex and they are going to make a man very happy one day if they have not already done that. Because I am in love with my wife, our sexual interactions and intimacy is so much more intense. Another man may not view my wife as the most beautiful woman that he has ever seen and he may not even feel that she is worth his time to approach (if she was not married), but I truly believe that my wife is the most beautiful woman that I have ever seen in person. Yes, it is because I am biased but not biased based on her being my wife, but biased based on her being the person that I am in love with. I have always thought that my wife was extraordinarily beautiful. The deeper in love I fall with her, the more attractive she is to me. It is still amazing to me that I am just as into her now, six years later, as I was when we started dating. One of the disgusting things about people (especially some men) is that no matter how beautiful, loving, caring, or faithful their partner may be, they tend to get bored and tired of seeing or being with the same person. In my early twenties, I was that way too. I was so set on being with this girl or that girl intimately because of her beauty and then after a month or two (sometimes less) my desire to be with her decreased significantly. The situation with my wife is totally different. I have been in love with her constantly for six years and my loving energy and desire for her has not decreased. You can have great *sex* and an addicting *sex-appeal* but without your partner being in love with you and vice versa, intimacy can only go so far.

Chapter 11 - YOUR FAMILY

I have heard people say that they don't care about having a healthy relationship with their partner's family. On one accord I can understand that. For me however, I was not willing to accept that as the case. If my wife's family would have been a bunch of negative nuts, I do not think I would be Makalia's husband.

As a teenager my friends talked about how much they loved and enjoyed their girlfriend's family. Quite a few of them admitted that the only reason they were dating their girlfriends for so long and maybe too long was because they had love and respect for her family. These discussions continued into my adulthood. When I began dating Makalia, who was my first real girlfriend in my adulthood, I understood what my guy friends were talking about. Makalia's family was for the most part warm, loving, accepting, and transparent with me. Her mother, sisters, aunts, and grandmother reminded me of the women in my family. Maybe they were *familiar spirits* too. They were also funny. I could be myself and they could be who they were and that was important to me. I remember dating a girl who caused me to feel degenerative about who I was. The only thing that really kept us together was our sexual and physical attraction to one another. I didn't enjoy her conversation, she devalued my opinions, and my family did not like her very much. Her family was congenial but we did not "click" and make a strong connection. Needless to say, that relationship did not last.

I have heard that married men typically prefer being around their wife's family for the holidays. I do not know if that is a greater myth than it is truth, but it has been the case for me during these first six years of my relationship. Not to say that my wife's family is any better to be around than my family. We get on each other's nerves the same way I do with my family but I think that my in-laws give me a little more space and I like that.

The only missing piece of the puzzle regarding my wife's family is her father. I was not privileged to have met her father because he passed away when she was younger. I have done some research on him, have heard stories about him, and I sometimes wonder what our relationship would have been like. Would he approve of me like the majority of her family does? Would he want to do some father and son-in-law activities like fishing, exercising, and watching sports? These are some of the things I wonder. The point being that your partner having an awesome family only makes your partner more appealing and attractive.

Chapter 12 - THE MAN HIMSELF

Does Mr. or Mrs. Right exist? Is there such a thing as the perfect match? I do not know the answer to these questions. As a man, or more-so as an individual, I constantly wonder why some women grouse about not being able to find a "good" man. *THE BOOK* tells us that "No one is good," (THE BOOK, 1996); but for the sake of things we will still use the word *good* for its common connotation. Though I do understand a woman's frustrations with men in general, I do not believe that some women have difficulty finding a good man. I believe some women have an arrogant self-image which inhibits them from taking an objective look at themselves and discerning some things they may be doing to push good men away. Saying that *there are no good men* takes the onus off of the author (the person making that claim) of that adage and now places it on someone else. It is easier to say that there is no "good" in the world than to take accountability and explore some of the things inside of oneself. Are men "dogs"? Some men are. Do all men cheat? No, some men cheat. Do all men beat their women? No, some men beat their women. Some women cheat too. Some women are "dogs"...*and cats*. Some women beat their men. Many women classify *all* men based on what *some* men do. Unconsciously, they create a disbelief in the fact that there are *other* men out there who do not do what *some* men do. Again, it is not a case of there being no good men out there. The real issue is that these non-believers have not been consistently exposed to higher quality men who are faithful in relationships and exhibit solidarity to high moral standards in their lives.

Another essential factor to think about is that the right man for you may not be currently living in your city or town. Too often I hear people claiming that they are not the "relationship type" because they have had too many failed relationships. When I ask who they have dated, they name people who live within a 5-10 mile radius. How can you limit finding your soul mate to the boundaries of your city or state? I once heard my great friend and spiritual brother, Darnell, say "When you look at a map of the world you can get an idea of how big God is. The problem is that most of us limit ourselves by not thinking outside of our own city." There are seven billion people on earth. It is highly likely that the person God has created to be the right person for you may be in another part of the world. Though I have a high amount of respect for the women I dated in Pittsburgh, I always had the belief that my potential wife was not from Pittsburgh. Go do some soul searching and soul mate searching!

Even if you meet your soul mate, how can you assess your future as a power couple? Since some women have not been raised by or consistently exposed to productive, loving, men of morale, it may be difficult to gather an idea about the qualities and characteristics that these types of men have. There are a multitude of factors that can be said regarding elements of a good man, but I would like to explore a few of the salient ones (from my perspective) to give you an idea of what to look for in your partner as well as what to prepare for and develop within yourself. Even if you find a partner with the following qualities and characteristics, you must be fit for them as much as you want them to be fit for you.

Let's take a look…

<u>FAMILY.</u>

People like to debate the argument of nature vs. nurture. Some people say we are who we are because of the nurture aspect while others lean towards the nature component. From my research and formal education, it appears to be half and half. I am who I am because God created me a certain way (my nature) but I have also been influenced by my family, friends, and other things (nurture). As I stated in the intro, I have not written this book to educate men and women on how to find a person exactly like my wife and me. My goal is to give you some themes and insight in regards to contributing to and helping you meet your life-partner. One of the ways you can assess someone and their potential as a life-partner is to meet, interact with, and research their family. This is not the same concept as the information within chapter 11. To enjoy your partner's family and to assess them are two different things. What I am saying and recommending here is that you do as much of an assessment, within reason, as you can about your partners family. (For example, do they have a history of health problems, criminal behavior, abuse, etc.?) How do they cope with familial problems? Assess other family dynamics such as present vs. absent figures in the home. Has your life-partner been raised by all women or a single father? I remember my first experience with my wife's family at her mother's house in St. Croix. Everyone was there; cousins, aunts, and her grandmother. (Her family, at the time, was not made up of a lot of men.) I offered to take the trash out and her mother, with a moderately aggressive tone stymied me saying, "No! Leave it there. We will get it." In my household, this was my responsibility because I was the boy but in Makalia's family the women did everything because there were mostly women in the family. This clash of family systems had a brief negative impact within our relationship once we moved in together. It is unlikely that your upbringing will perfectly complement your partner's upbringing but my point is that you need to make the assessment early in the relationship in order to figure out what kinks may need to be ironed out.

You should also look at your partner's mother, father, sisters and brothers and assess their appearance. Do not necessarily look for beauty. Assess their hygiene and style. Do they take care of themselves? This may be an indication of what your life-partner may look like in the next 15-25+ years.

Respectfully assess as much as possible; education, interests, financial stability, children, etc. More importantly, as you assess these things, look for themes. If all the adults in your partner's family are on their third or fourth marriage this may be an important theme to take into account.

WHAT HE/SHE SAW GROWING UP.

We have discussed the impact of family and the influence they have on us. Unlike "The Truman Show" you will not be able to ask your partners parents for a video that captures their entire upbringing. However, it is of salient necessity that you have a respectful curiosity about why your partner is the way he or she is. For example, I have always been a neat freak and I have always liked to cook. These are things that I get from my father. I grew up seeing a six foot five alpha male waking up at 4:00 am to wash clothes, make lunch for my sisters and me, and cook dinner for later in the day. He did all of this and had it completed by 6:00 am. My dad did this every day; *this is what I saw* growing up. This is why I believe I am very self-sufficient. When I first met my wife and she began coming over to my apartment, she was amazed at how clean it was. Later on in our relationship she told me she thought I had another woman coming over to clean my apartment.

I also saw my dad cooking for people who came over the house, engaging in conversation with them and offering solutions to problems in different areas of their lives. My dad has always been someone people love, enjoy, and respect because he has a daunting presence with a kind personality. My mother has had a great impact on me as well. She interacted with me a lot and developed my humorous side. She wrestled with me and she was a damn good wrestler. I probably learned how to fight because of her. I could not pin her until I was 15 years old. Can you believe that? It's the truth! These are some things I saw growing up that contributed to some of my own idiosyncrasies and attributes.

No family is perfect or has a life without some traumatic experiences. I have been blessed to have great parents. Not only was I raised by an alpha male but my mother is an alpha female. They both have strong personalities and when they spoke, people listened. Sometimes, it was because of the fear-factor. My parents both grew up being the intimidators and fighters in their communities. I never saw them physically fight each other and they did not harm people in front of us but that does not mean their aggressive nature left them. My parents were always nice people but they did not hesitate to exercise their aggressive nature and violent capabilities on others if and when needed. I did experience mild forms of their aggression through whippings and verbal threats. Most of my whippings were deserved. I do not agree with some of the ways in which they used their verbiage but that was their style and I had to respect it. I would have rather taken the whippings than the derogatory comments. My mother's words would cut deep and my father's words combined with his deep, loud voice would shake the ground and make us all nervous. My goal is not to insinuate that my parents abused me in any way. My goal is to say that I picked up on the good, the bad, and some of the traumatic things I witnessed growing up. For example, I am kind hearted like my father, I am funny like my mother, and I am self-sufficient like the both of them. I cannot shy away from the fact that I can be as aggressive and dangerous as I can be peaceful. I know how to use my words and fists like bullets. I am not proud of this but this is part of who I am because of *what I saw*. My wife has had to do a lot of reconditioning of my thinking via her *conversation* to let me know that I do not have to respond to people with aggression whenever they do things I don't like. She has continually encouraged me to use my words to build people up and not break them down. She has not changed me but she has offered me other solutions to counter some of the negative things I saw and did growing up.

My wife also saw some things growing up. She has been traumatized by the passing of her king, her father. I did not know her then but I doubt that she is the same person now as she was before. Though we are respectful of one another's situation, it has been a struggle for us both to deal with each other's behaviors that are a direct response to what we saw growing up.

I would love to believe that my wife and I would still desire to be together back in 2008 knowing what we know now about each other but only God knows what would happen in that situation. This is why I have written this book; for you to use our hindsight as your foresight. As you begin or continue to look into the future of your own relationship, you may have some tough questions to explore. *"Can I deal with him being a control freak like his dad?, Can I deal with her running her mouth and talking so much like her mother?, How will he/she deal with me being a workaholic, etc."* Of course people can change over the course of time but we do not know if and when that time will come. Any partner (even your soul mate) is going to be a gamble but it is wise to do your research on your significant other before risking it all.

Chapter 13 - DIVINE INTERVENTION

I believe the previous chapters entail some the most prominent elements it takes to procure your dream partner. I also believe that if you explore these ideas in a way that relates to you as an individual and assimilate them into your life, your chances of picking your dream partner will significantly increase. We must not forget that the plans we have for ourselves are not necessarily the plans that God has for us. For example, you might use the ideas from this book, recommendations from other books, do everything right and still not find your dream partner. Sometimes...probably more often than not, it takes *divine intervention* to make things work. That is what it took for me. Back in 2008 when I met my wife, I was not using all the information I give you within this book. I was not that sophisticated yet. My wife's entrance into my life was literally divine intervention.

On August 31, 2008 I was chilling in my apartment with my friend Chris and a couple college basketball teammates; laughing and joking over some drinks. It was a Sunday night and they wanted to go out. It was getting late, I had to work the next morning and I didn't want to leave my place, but after a prolonged campaign they convinced me to go out. We went to a place in Pittsburgh called *S Bar*. We walked in and I immediately saw a group of girls dancing in the VIP section. My friends and I noticed them noticing us, but we played it cool and went to the bar to get some drinks. About 15 minutes later one of the girls left VIP and approached me. It was Makalia. I do not remember the conversation verbatim but she said that my response to her was so aggressive and inappropriate that she immediately felt that approaching me was not the right decision. She walked away, my friends and I ordered one more round of drinks and then left. I did not get her number and she did not ask for mine. I left with my crew and we tried to find other bars/clubs to go to but it was futile. It was Sunday night in Pittsburgh, there was not much to do so we went back to S Bar. As soon as we walked back in, Makalia was standing by the door dancing with her girls. She came up to me, took my cell phone, put her number in my phone, and that is how our relationship began. I know they say you shouldn't *wife a chick from the club* but she turned out to be an anomaly. She was a young lady.

When I was a kid I saw images in my sleep of a woman walking on a beach in a sundress. I saw this woman often throughout my childhood nighttime dreams. Makalia and I got married in St. Croix, Virgin Islands (on a beach) where she is from and when I looked at our wedding pictures for the first time it hit me, this was her! This was the woman I saw walking on the beach when I was a kid! It was at that moment I realized that when I left S Bar the first time on August 31, 2008 I had almost walked out on the women of my dreams. What brought me back to her was *divine intervention*.

I thank you for sharing these moments of your life with me and I hope reading this book has been worth your time. As you process the information and figure out how to apply it to your life, I'd like to encourage you not to try to control everything on your path towards and within your relationship. <u>Let go and let God</u>...I pray that you and your soul mate find one another in peace and love.

You can reach me at www.PerspectVe.com. Remember to spell the word PerspectVe without the "i" because to broaden your own horizons, sometimes you have to take yourself out of your own PerspectVe. Take care and I pray you a happy, healthy, and meaningful life of success and fulfillment through God.

References

THE BOOK. (1996). Wheaton, Illinois: Tyndale House Publishers, Inc.

ARLENE F. HARDER, M. M. (2011). Retrieved Februrary 15, 2014, from SUPPORT4CHANGE.COM: http://www.support4change.com/index.php?option=com_content&view=article&id=47&Itemid=108

Made in the USA
Monee, IL
30 March 2023

30670141R10039